My Spouse Wants More Sex Than Me

The 2- Minute Solution for a Happier Marriage

Ruxandra LeMay, Psy.D.

Table of Contents

Preface

Why write *The 2-Minute Solution*? Well, at first, because my husband insisted on it. I can't tell you how many times we have argued over whether this book will make a difference. In his mind, he is fighting on behalf of all the married men who are possibly misunderstood and sexually and emotionally deprived, and he strongly believes that this book will help many.

Interestingly enough, while the psychologist in me totally agrees with him, the female part of my brain continues to side with the stereotypical question: "Why does he care about sex that much?" This is kind of crazy, because I didn't have this question when we first started dating. Honestly, I probably would have felt confused if he hadn't cared about sex back then.

How did it all start? Well, we have been together for seventeen years and married for twelve years. We definitely think of our relationship in BC and AC terms - that is, "before and after children." Our children are the most amazing people in our lives, and we are a hundred times happier and more content since they were born. They are also the reason for a lot of changes in our lives.

Before children, our lives consisted of work, lots of spontaneous date nights, movie marathons, and a whole lot more adrenaline between the sheets.

After children, our lives consist of getting dressed, making breakfast, packing lunches, getting dressed (did I say that already? That's because I'll bet one of us is not dressed yet), brushing teeth, driving kids to school, picking kids up from school, doing homework, taking kids to sports practice, getting dinner ready, feeding everyone, washing everyone, reading stories, and getting ready for the next day. Did we feed the dogs? How about the turtles? Or the fish? Are we done for today? Because I just want to get some sleep before we do it all over again tomorrow. A few years ago, there was a mom on YouTube who could sing her entire daily routine in one minute. Back then, when I was single, I thought she was weird. Today, I am that mother.

On the rare occasions when I go out to Happy Hour with my girlfriends, also mothers, we compare notes about our kids, about our spouses, and most often about how tired we are. And with that, occasionally we laugh about how our intimate lives have changed. Because I am a fairly private person, I am not quite ready to dive into specific details about how my sex life has evolved in the last eight years, but let's just say that it has morphed into something a lot less steamy and romantic and a lot more practical.

This brings us to how the idea behind this book was born. Fortunately, while all of these changes were taking place, I was also getting a graduate degree in psychology. Both my husband and I agree that psychology kept us together, helped us grow, and allowed us to truly learn about each other.

As a child of divorced parents, I have developed an interest in how relationships start, maintain, and end, so it was a natural progression to focus on couples' therapy during my graduate studies. Over time, I have gathered a lot of notes from the hundreds of books and articles, hours of therapy work with clients, and conversations with friends and relatives, and I have used many quotes and ideas from these sources in my writing.

Although there are a number of good books on sex, marriage, and communication, I have always found that most of the couples' books are too long, are too complex, and try to cover too many intricate aspects of a relationship. Many readers get lost in all of the information and have a difficult time finding areas of focus or ideas that could be immediately applied to day-to-day life, so they can experience the much-needed relief in a timely manner.

Becoming a wife and a mother helped me develop a different and much better way of understanding and relating to my clients than any of the theories covered in graduate school. I realized that most of these books, although great resources, are often difficult to implement when your daily routine is as chaotic as I described earlier. Thus, I have tried to simplify the process of marital therapy to five key elements: sex, communication, financial matters, parenting, and dealing with in-laws (extended family).

This book will cover only two of these areas: *sex* and *communication*. I generally believe that if spouses are able to manage these two areas, they will have a significantly easier time working out the others.

I won't lie. Marriage is hard. Once the blinding lust is gone, marriage is work. It is about constant compromise, scheduling, taking turns, sharing, and giving up personal likes for the benefit of the children and the integrity of the relationship. And even if you manage to get all of this right, there isn't a guarantee that the relationship will survive. It ultimately comes down to the ability of each spouse to let go, as well as the partners' level of optimism, sense of humor, and degree of commitment.

Obviously, when a marriage becomes work (and it will), the quantity and quality of sex change. This is not my opinion; this is just a fact of life. It simply depends on how much it changes. If it disappears or if it becomes the topic of excruciatingly painful daily conversations, you and/or your spouse have to do something about it, if you want the relationship to survive.

My straightforward approach to sex in a marriage has often been called "unromantic" or "too pragmatic." There is some truth to this, but I prefer to describe my method as "a commonsense, easy-to-implement, and effective approach to a challenging time in a couple's life." And it works.

My Spouse Wants More Sex Than Me: The 2- Minute Solution for a Happier Marriage is a self-help book about sex and communication in a marriage. It is a humorous and straightforward book that talks about the reality of a marital relationship, not about the fairy tale you see in movies. With this book, I hope to:

- First and foremost, challenge the traditional mind-set that good sex has to last for at least thirty minutes of foreplay, thirty minutes of penetration, and thirty minutes of cuddling.

- Share the truth about the differences between men and women in terms of sex drive, desire, and arousal.

- Offer a solution for the times when these differences widen, such as illness, stress, or being busy with work and parenthood.

- Help spouses understand each other's experience and find the time, energy, and motivation for sex in a crazy and fast-paced day-to-day routine.

I am sure you have already picked up from the tone of the book that women (especially busy, tired mothers) are less interested in sex. And although this statement is true for many, many women and is the focus of this book, I also want to make it clear that I am not generalizing and I am not saying that this is every woman's experience.

The truth, however, is that most women nowadays work full-time jobs, still take care of the children and the household, and sometimes help care for ailing parents, relatives, or friends. Most women who are physically, mentally, and emotionally drained from juggling all of these tasks just don't have the energy or motivation to have sex.

Nonetheless, this is not one of those books that tell you it's your job to keep your man happy. It's not going to tell you to buy sexy lingerie, how to find anyone's secret G-spot, how to give mind-blowing oral sex, or how to have one-hour-long orgasms several times a night. You can find that advice in each of the last five hundred issues of *Cosmopolitan* or *Glamour* magazine. Most likely, you already know how to do most of those things. Most likely you used to do some of these things. But today, that is such a thought of the past. Today, the only thing you are looking forward to is watching a few episodes of *Scandal*, snuggling with a good book and a glass of wine after the kids are asleep, or getting a full nine-hour beauty sleep.

In all fairness, I also know women who struggle with the extreme opposite situation: their husbands are not interested in sex. Although the core of this book is directed toward women with lower sex drive-related issues, the ideas in this book are very much applicable to both scenarios; thus, both men and women could benefit from reading it.

As a matter of fact, for best results, I encourage you to read this book with your partner. Reading this book together is an opportunity to find out how you both feel about the topic and to understand each other's perspective. Furthermore, it is an opportunity to learn that you are not alone. The experience of whatever is happening (or not happening) in your marriage is shared by many, many other couples. That insight in itself is often therapeutic.

However, the most important part is that *The 2-Minute Solution* is a **hands-on book** that strongly encourages **practice**. No self-help book, no matter how great it is, will make a difference unless the readers are willing to practice the skills described. To help with the practice aspect of this book, I have included "The Insight Corner" at the end of each chapter. This box describes a variety of assignments that are supposed to make you think about, talk about, and do things that may be out of your comfort zone, but are great stepping-stones for change. Please remember that practice takes time and failure before one can experience long-lasting success.

Those who know me can vouch that I am a big believer in "practice what you preach," so I can say that my husband and I have been working at these skills for about seven years. I won't lie; it did take some work, but this work was worth the time and effort. And don't get me wrong, these skills and ideas will not resolve all of your marital problems, and they will not prevent arguments from happening. As a matter of fact, we still experience ups and downs that make me doubt my expert status at times, but, overall, we have made it so far, and we still like each other.

Please keep in mind that I wrote this book to complement and not to replace other medical, pharmacological, psychological, and spiritual resources available for couples' health and marital therapy. There will be times when it is recommended to consult your physician, a sex therapist, your pastor, a friend, or a relative on the thousands of things that could go wrong (or right) in your relationship. I wrote this book, however, to stimulate a different perspective.

The thoughts and sex-provoking ideas described in this book have helped many, but they may not be helpful to all. While I am a licensed psychologist with experience in couples' therapy, I am not a physician or a licensed sex therapist. Please consult with a physician, especially if you have a condition that may affect your sexual endeavors.

Finally, just to cross this off the list and ward off all of the critics who may line up to say that this book will take women back to the dark ages, this is not about a "wife's duty to perform" or about some sort of submissive perspective. I meant this book to be a modern and fresh "hands-on" approach (no pun intended) to highlight how biology, communication, and psychology can come together successfully and contribute to a loving and committed relationship in today's fast-paced and often stressful home environment.

1

Once Upon a Time, We Used to Have Sex

"I want it bad. Can't wait until your hands are all over my body tonight."

If this is a thought you had and communicated to your husband recently and meant every word of it, congratulations, keep doing what you are doing! But if this is a line you barely remember from ten years ago, keep reading this book.

I'll bet that ten years ago, you could not wait for his call. You still remember the first kiss, the first touch, and the first night together. Any time apart was unbearable, and, in fact, you read every sex article in *Cosmo* because you really wanted to have sex all the time. You wanted to make him want you more. You wanted to be the only one who would get his attention. You, of course, were in **Stage One** of the relationship.

Throughout the book, I will review and refer to these "stages of a relationship" and will try to show you the connections between your thoughts, feelings, and actions as time passes and your relationship matures. Children go through identifiable growth stages, new products have development phases, and so do romantic relationships. Although the stages of a relationship have been studied and described by many experts in the field, I like Dr. Helen Fisher's simple description of the process. Dr. Fisher is a biological anthropologist whose interest in gender differences and the evolution of human sex, love, and relationships have led her to do extensive research and writing on these topics.

In her book *Why We Love* (2004), Dr. Fisher states that over time, people have developed three basic brain systems for mating: lust, romantic love, and attachment. Although most people undergo these areas in this specific order, some don't. Some have sex first, and then they fall in love. Others are friends first, and then they have sex. For the purpose of this book, we will follow the traditional course of a relationship.

I can't stress enough how important it is for people to understand that this process or evolution in a relationship is perfectly normal and happens to most people, if not all, in one form or another. When we start a relationship or a marriage, we somehow expect the fairy tale and the passion to last forever. Although at some level, we know that's not true, we'll always imagine that "the lows cannot be that low for us" because, unlike other people, we are "soul mates" and "we have true love."

When it comes to relationships, I like to look at the big picture before I start focusing on the details. Therefore, I make it a habit to review these normal changes in the course of a relationship during the first few sessions of any couples' therapy. My clients' first reaction is often one of relief as they are reassured that <u>these changes happen to everyone</u>. Of course, what makes a difference between successful marriages and failed ones is ***<u>how we react to and how we handle these changes</u>***.

Lustful Love

So, let's go back to the beginning. As I mentioned, **Stage One**, aka **Lustful Love**, is an all-consuming, overwhelming time characterized by strong biased feelings of falling in love, magnetic sexual desire and gratification, a removal of boundaries, and imagining the other as perfect. This is often based on biological drives, rather than on rational thoughts. It is about a basic drive to get close, to procreate, and to get sexual gratification. Hormones such as <u>estrogen</u> and <u>testosterone</u> create amazing feelings of butterflies, tingling, shortness of breath, and excitement (Fisher et al., 2002).

In addition, a higher level of the neurotransmitter <u>dopamine</u> creates intense energy, exhilaration, and focused attention. This is the same neurotransmitter that is affected by cocaine and most other drugs. This explains why, when you are newly in love, you can stay up all night, hike a mountain faster, and push the limits of your skills.

Such an intense physical and emotional craving to be with this person can make you completely obsessed, to the point where you spend most of your time thinking about him or her. And of course, as we all know, the sex is amazing. Interestingly enough, <u>during this first stage, sex is amazing for most people, even the ones who are diagnosed with low desire or another sexual dysfunction at later stages of a relationship</u>.

However, our brains are always altering. With every new experience, bit of new learning, and new social connection, our brains experience small and subtle changes. Our brains are not wired to keep up with this constant high level of arousal. Research studies show that these hormones drop back to normal levels after twelve to sixteen months of being in a relationship. Because it is impossible to maintain that level of intensity, most individuals will experience changes in their relationships.

Romantic Love

This leads us into **Stage Two**, aka **Romantic Love.** Hormonal love will eventually come to an end. Imagine what would happen if your significant other was your top priority, day in and day out. I'll bet you'd never get anything else done. Being totally immersed in each other feels great and leads to some great sex, but it is exhausting and unproductive. The reality is that humans are wired for survival and not for having hot sex all day long.

Furthermore, it is difficult to keep up the mask of perfection. During Stage One, we are all on our best behavior because we want to impress our love interest. But by Stage Two, we are more inclined to express our true thoughts, feelings, and interests. We see our partner's negative characteristics more and more clearly, and even more scarily, they see ours. First arguments take place. First doubts cross our minds. Rather than focusing only on the idea of "us" as a new couple, people start oscillating between individuality and togetherness.

Of course, it is difficult to remember and accept that this other person is a separate individual with his or her own thoughts, feelings, beliefs, and behaviors, after we were immersed in each other during Stage One. Yet, if the couple is able to reconcile and survive the first waves of differences and disagreements, the partners usually come out stronger, often feeling as if they belong together and are part of the same team. This time, there is a craving for emotional union with the partner.

It is at this point that people consider taking the relationship to a new level because they want to share their lives together forever, during good times and bad times. Although sex is not as intense, it is still passionate, and it's complemented by a strong feeling of belonging. The brain acquires a tolerance to the love stimulants and starts to release another neurotransmitter, the endorphins (Fisher, 2004). Endorphins are natural opiates that calm the nerves, relieve pain, and lower stress. They are the same chemicals released after a good workout, and they strongly contribute to a general sense of well-being.

This stage typically lasts from sixteen to about thirty-six months. Of course, some people don't make it past this stage, but those who do, will get the ring, buy the white dress magazines, and start preparing for the big wedding, all of which are just the beginning of a promising journey together.

These are fun stages. Both people are full of love, compassion, and caring with a strong focus on sexual expression and experimentation. Although mutual interest, hobbies, and life philosophies are the glue that will make up the friendship aspect of the relationship, *it is truly the physical attraction and the sex that make the partners more than just roommates.*

The Insight Corner

List the top 5 qualities about your spouse that caught your attention while you were dating.

1._____

2._____

3._____

4._____

5._____

2
Marriage, Parenthood, and Sex

Fred: It's Friday night, the kids are asleep, and we finally get some time together.

Susan: I'm sorry, I had a long day, I just ate, I'm tired and have to get up early tomorrow for Johnny's soccer game. But we'll do it later, I promise.

Fred: That's what you said last weekend; that's what you've been saying for a month.

Susan: Is sex all that you're thinking about? It's like you never get enough. Do you have an addiction or something?

Fred: No, I don't think so, but I love you and want to be with you. Or, maybe I am addicted to you. We used to have sex all the time. The question is: why aren't you interested in having sex with me? Are you not attracted to me? Are you cheating on me? Is there something wrong with you? Maybe you should get checked out.

Does this sound like the current theme in your house? I know this rings a bell to me and many other women who are brave enough to admit it. Of course, this is not a conversation you had ten years ago, but it is a fairly typical conversation for where you are now: married with children.

To highlight this change in our relationship, I like to quote Esther Perel's work. As an outsider to American society, Esther grew up in Europe and lived and worked in many countries, where she was exposed to a wide variety of sexual attitudes and practices. So, yes, her work is a lot more liberal than what you would usually find in American mainstream literature, and, therefore, it is a great avenue for those looking for unbiased sexual exploration.

In her book *Erotic Intelligence* (2003), she states: "It always amazes me how much people are willing to experiment sexually outside their relationships, yet how tame and puritanical they are at home with their partners. Domestic sex lives devoid of excitement and eroticism, yet are consumed and aroused by a richly imaginative sexual life beyond domesticity-affairs, pornography, day dreams."

We may hate to admit it, but it is often very true. Yet, although it is true, this is because the relationship is changing, it is evolving, and it is changing its purpose.

Let me explain by first going back to the stages of a relationship. We have looked at the Lustful Love and the Romantic Love stages. Next comes **Stage Three,** aka **Attached Love,** otherwise called marriage.

Marriage

Now, the fairy-tale wedding is over. Spouses have opened all of the wedding presents, kitchen utensils, towels, and cookware, and they slowly get settled into their blissful marriage. They may decide they are ready to buy a house, a couple of dogs, and some fish, and finally have kids. All of these are great additions to their lives. Yet, as fun as these sound on paper, they all require additional time, energy, and emotional commitment. As the spouses' energy gets spread thinner and thinner, they have less time for each other. They also have less physical and emotional availability for each other.

The reality is that as we get secure in the relationship and get comfortable with each other, we are also inclined to pay attention to other areas of our lives. These are areas of life that were important to us prior to the start of the relationship, but that were put on hold because sex hormones and the process of mating took over most of our brains. Now that we've been in the same relationship for a couple of years and feel secure in our relationship, bound by marital vows and a legal contract, we go back to focusing on pursuing an education, a career, a better job, old friendships, family relationships, hobbies, or, as the relationship continues, parenthood.

What Is Habituation?

Likewise, biology kicks in again. Sex with the same person, just like any other activity, is a repetitive activity. Yes, we can spice it up with some different positions, and toys, or by acting out fantasies, but after a few years, things can get plainly routine and unexciting. There is nothing wrong with our partners. They are the same people we used to have hot sex with; maybe with a few extra pounds, but nothing that can't be fixed. There is also nothing wrong with us. Yet, the brain may play mind tricks on all of us and make us believe something is wrong.

Our brains undergo the process of *habituation*. Habituation is a decrease in response to a stimulus after repeated presentations. In plain English, our brains get used to the same repetitive action, and more important, the brain knows what to expect. There are no surprises as we would have with a new person. This process is so important to understand, because it can cause confusion and it can trick us into believing that there is something wrong with the relationship.

Think about your favorite food, think about its smell, how it looks on the plate, and the atmosphere at your favorite restaurant. I'll bet you are starting to salivate a little. Now think about having that delicious, exciting, and maybe expensive meal every day. I can guarantee that after a week, a month, let alone, one year, you'll be completely sick of it. The same concept applies to being around the same person and having sex with the same person or, as a matter of fact, doing anything else over and over again with the same person.

Ironically, most individuals who are attracted to the idea of marriage are also attracted to the ideal of safety, reliability, and predictability. A lot of us crave it and need it in order to function or feel complete. Yet, when we sign the marital contract, we are not really aware of the fact that these come at the expense of excitement, mystery, and erotic fascination. Unfortunately, "erotic passion is defiant and unpredictable, unruly and undependable. Where nothing is forbidden, nothing is erotic" (Perel, 2003). And this is very much applicable to both men and women.

"Safe" and "Hot" Don't Co-Exist

As you dive deeper into each of these ideas, you'll realize that we are talking about two seemingly unrelated worlds. It's like watching *Everybody Loves Raymond* vs. *9 1/2 Weeks*. Can you imagine Patricia Heaton blind-folded and licking strawberries out of Mickey Rourke's hands? That movie is so old and yet so hot, still. Anyway, I got sidetracked. Yes, at one point or another, we all crave and badly miss the carnal, passionate, devouring kiss between Basinger and Rourke...because in reality, nowadays, all we get or give are pecks on the cheek as we pass each other in the morning, like two ships in the night.

What happened to us? I know we still love each other. Well, biologically, it appears that couples in long-term relationships move from a dopamine- or endorphin-dominant state of passionate love to a safe oxytocin- and vasopressin-dominant attachment. Oxytocin and vasopressin are neuropeptides that are associated with feelings of bonding and connection and are released during breastfeeding, hugging, and holding. "Safe" feels good, but it's not really exciting. "Safe" does not really invite a whole lot of sex or it allows for some sex, only it's dull and routine sex.

Sex is just not as much of a priority as it used to be. Life has a tendency to settle into a routine as we get busy with earning a paycheck, washing dishes, chasing the kids, paying the bills, cleaning pets' vomit off the carpet, and tolerating the in-laws. Although most people still experience some level of sex drive, it is often diminished, and it is inconsistent. This applies even more to women than to men. For example, the woman may feel like having hot, passionate sex once in a while (usually around ovulation time, because hormones change again) but not may not feel as if she needs any sex at all in between. Men's sex drive, conversely, is more consistent and typically a lot higher.

These two worlds grow even further apart once the spouses become parents. Actually, from a sociological perspective, Dr. Fisher hypothesized that Stage Three, Attached Love, evolved over time with the sole purpose of enabling males and females to tolerate a mate long enough to complete species-specific parental duties. This sounds really gloomy, the complete opposite of the fairy tale we signed up for when we said "I do," but it often turns out to be true.

Pregnancy - The Total Game Changer

What's also true is that pregnancy and parenting are truly game changers in the relationship, with both spouses experiencing tremendous fluctuations in their sexual practices.

For example, the average man does not find it easy or appealing to see his wife gain forty pounds or more, become an irrational emotional roller-coaster with making odd demands at various hours of the day and night, be unable to move off the couch, complain of hemorrhoids and gas, scream her head off as if she were being tortured by enemy combatants during the delivery and expunge a baby and a pound of bloody placenta through the same venue that used to be the object of the man's oral fixation.

On the note of oral fixation, the other two objects, her breasts, become devices borrowed from a country farm that are either attached to a starving baby or to a machine that pulls and tugs for every drop of milk.

Please, don't get me wrong, it's not that I am unsympathetic or unaware of how painful this experience is for women (I have been there three times, and I was not a happy pregnant woman). Yet, it is definitely not fair to be in complete denial about how all of this could affect a man's interest in sex or, even worse, to tell him " You shouldn't feel this way." Now, the good news is that for most men, this becomes ancient history in about six to twelve months. Most, although not all, men are able to recover their sex drive and performance in a fairly timely manner.

For women, this is not as easy. The body changes during the pregnancy, the labor and delivery, and the post-partum period are enough to make us erase sex off the list completely for at least one year (especially after the first child). And, it does not stop there.

Motherhood

Becoming a mother is an overwhelming, everlasting sensory transformation. I can't stress this enough. Ms. Perel does a beautiful job of describing this experience. In her article, "When Three Threatens Two" (2006), she explains how the same senses that used to be utilized for sex, although no longer used for sexual gratification, are now fully employed for a completely different function, as we become an extension of our babies. "We caress their silky skin, we kiss, we cradle, we rock. We nibble their toes, they touch our faces, they breastfeed. This blissful fusion resembles the physical connection between lovers."

Of course, the woman does not feel one ounce of sexuality, and she obviously cannot be turned instantly just because her husband enters the room. Being around their babies or kids is an all-consuming, exhausting, and equally fulfilling experience for many mothers. "At the end of the day, there is nothing left to give but there may be also nothing more that she needs" (Perel, 2006). She doesn't need anything from her spouse because she is so content from holding and cuddling her baby.

I'll admit that I can fully relate to this experience. When I first met my husband, nothing could keep me away from him. I never thought I would experience a bigger love than that. And then, I had kids. Cuddling with my kids, touching their hair, kissing them, wrestling with them on the floor, holding them when they cry or get sick, all of that is the best feeling in the entire world, and nothing makes me feel more complete. Being away from them for more than one night is physically and mentally painful. This is exactly how I felt about my husband when we were dating, but fifteen years later, it seems as if my children totally hold my heart.

Depending on each couple's approach to parenting and the level of attachment to their children, this experience may continue for up to ten years, as parents and children often cuddle and share the bed at night until the kids are ready to separate on their own. Although, as the kids go to school and the mothers get some space, they are usually able to detach, find themselves, and re-experience sexual moments, most parents go for a second or third child during this time span, so the cycle starts all over again, leaving very little physical, emotional, or sexual energy for their spouses.

One mom said to me once, "I would rather snuggle with my kids than my husband most days. I feel bad that I don't have a desire to be with him, but not bad enough to change it. He definitely feels like I don't care for him or that I am not attracted to him, which is not the case." She is certainly not the minority.

The good news is that most women will be able to recapture some of their femininity and sexual interest in time, especially as the kids get older and become more independent. This should offer some comfort to them, as well as to their spouses. The women will become interested in their looks, their hair, their make-up, and their general appearance. They will want to look sexy and appealing again. And with that, some of their initial sexual friskiness may return.

However, there is also a good possibility that despite recapturing their sexy selves, many women may still not have a dire need for sexual contact or intimacy. In the meantime, the husband, who never stopped needing the closeness and the sexual release, will be completely dismayed to realize that his wife still doesn't want sex. After he waited patiently for months and perhaps years, nothing changes. This can create an immense rift in the marriage.

This brings me to the solution you've been looking for, and this is what I, unromantically but effectively, call *the 2-minute solution*. It is a great bridge for these times. It is a great compromise. It allows women to find themselves, and enjoy their sensory experience with their children without completely sacrificing the sexual connection with their spouses. It allows men to enjoy their spouses sexually without having to apologize for their sex drive. It is my way of saying: "Don't let your lack of desire become a roadblock to a happy and healthy marriage."

The Insight Corner

How have children changed your sex life? How do you feel about it? How does your spouse feel about it?

_____

_____

_____

_____

3
Sexual Gridlock

"Sex is the price women have to pay for marriage, and marriage is the price men have to pay for sex."

(Anonymous)

Pretty bold statement! Some may find it outdated and offensive. I find it funny and a little true!

Think about it: historically, women have been interested in the security of a sound and reliable marital relationship for the purpose of raising their children. Yes, most women nowadays are interested in having sex in the beginning of the relationship, and, thanks to the female sexual revolution, women can be adventurous, have fun, and express themselves. However, the sexual revolution never changed the fact once the marital contract is signed and children come along, female sexuality changes significantly.

Yet, historically, men have been socialized to be the ones pursuing women with wine, food, flowers, and jewelry, with the ultimate prize of having sex. They may not admit it, but they all think it at some point: if there is no sex in the relationship, what's the point of being in an intimate relationship? Without sex, you could be just roommates.

Thus, as the relationship changes, how do you reconcile a naturally occurring lower sex drive of a woman with a naturally occurring higher sex drive of a man?

In other words, as a wife, how many times has your husband nagged you into sex? And how many times, have you said NO to him? I have been there, my girlfriends have been there, and I can't tell you how many times I have heard this scenario in couples' therapy.

In his book *Passionate Marriage*, Dr. David Schnarch does a great job of describing the process he calls *marital sexual gridlock* (Schnarch, 2009). He states that the harder a man tries to increase the female's desire, the less power he has. His frequent invitations make her even more unreceptive. Generally speaking, a woman can have all the sex she wants, when she wants it, without trying too hard. And because the ball is in her court, the male is totally dependent on what the female wants. The more the male demands it, the less she wants to have it or to be with him.

The reality of a monogamous relationship is that the person with the least amount of desire controls the sex. Otherwise, it would be called rape. So, generally speaking and for the purpose of this book, the woman is in control of the sex department. Yet, what a woman doesn't realize is that every time she says NO, she is conditioning the male to pester her. Aside from "rewarding" him every time he complains, she is teaching him what really motivates her.

She doesn't have sex out of desire; she has it when he gets her to feel sufficiently guilty and frustrated or when she starts to feel afraid he may not want her and may look for a replacement.

> "The only time I seem to want sex is when he finally stops asking for it."

Sadly, the partner with a higher sex drive is always dependent on the other one and often opens himself up for a lot of rejection. Although it's not always the case, most of the time, the partner with a higher sex drive is the husband.

I know men have the reputation of "thinking about sex every twenty seconds," "thinking with their penis," "being interested only in their own physical pleasure," or "being interested only in sex and beer." This may be true all the time for some men, and it may be true sometimes for the rest of the male population. But I also know from my schooling, my therapy sessions with men, my own relationship, and raising boys that these are not the main reasons why men need to have physical attention from their spouses.

How Does a Man Feel?

Just like women, men need love, warmth, closeness, validation, and acceptance. Men are also more physical (due to a higher level of testosterone), and they express these needs for emotional closeness by doing things side by side with their wives. It could be walking together, gardening together, eating together, or, their favorite, having sex together. When sex is not an option in a marriage, it throws them off not only physically but also emotionally.

Although women assume that men are used to this kind of rejection, please use this as a reminder that rejection is never pleasant. When a man is rejected by the partner he loves for days, weeks, or years, it also takes a significant toll on his self-esteem and emotional well-being.

When men feel a stronger interest in, and need for, sexual intimacy, they will speak up at first. When that turns out to be unproductive, it turns into nagging. Yet when his nagging leads to the wife's blow-up, he is left with only two choices: shutting down or acting out.

On a day-to-day basis, <u>shutting down</u> may look something like this: not paying attention to the surroundings (such as the wife or the kids), focusing only on work, working overtime, not participating in household chores, spending most of his free time on the computer or watching TV, and choosing to spend time with friends, even when his spouse needs help at home.

Shutting down also happens because it is physically painful for a man to be attracted to or turned on by his wife but not be able to touch her. He has to shut down his senses to co-exist with her under the same roof without walking around frustrated and angry all the time (which may still happen).

<u>Acting out</u>, conversely, may look like irritability, anger, and aggression with you or the kids, overeating, overdrinking, spending too much money, watching too much porn, paying attention to other women, and even having extramarital affairs.

Most men go back and forth between the two

styles, hoping that it will get the spouse's attention and resolve something in the relationship. Unfortunately, if the couple doesn't get to the bottom of the core problem, unsatisfied physical urges and lack of emotional intimacy, not much will be resolved.

Another way to look at this, especially if you have boys, is to think back when they were babies, toddlers, and teenagers. At every stage and with every milestone, they needed attention, reassurance, and love. They needed and wanted to be hugged, kissed, and cuddled. Not any different from girls, as a matter of fact.

Yet for some reason, we expect men (who are just a bigger version of our sons) to drop these needs and wants and to be happy in a long-term monogamous relationship without satisfying their basic needs. Does that sound fair?

How Does a Woman Feel?

Women who have been socialized to be sex symbols and take care of their man's needs, however, understand the importance of sex in a relationship, but they have a difficult time reconciling their own needs (significantly lower) with their spouses'. They often feel guilty and even angry that they are not interested in sex; they feel as if they are not satisfying their significant others, that there is something wrong with them, and that they are the only ones with this problem.

Yet often they will not admit that they are not interested in sex or not interested in sex lasting a long time because that would mean they are "less of a woman." In the first phase, they will give reasons, such as exhaustion (a very valid one), headaches or other physical issues, or chores, just to get out of having sex.

When those excuses don't work anymore, women may get aggressive and start picking on the husband needing so much sex or, they make accusations, saying that there is something wrong with their husbands in an attempt to make the men feel guilty. At times, women will even focus on the spouses' negative or annoying traits and use those as a reason for their diminished interest. Such a dynamic will likely lead to more fights, which, of course, will result in no sex. In the long run, this vicious cycle is a recipe for a miserable marriage or even divorce.

Interestingly enough, I did notice another pattern. If the husband stops asking for sex and shows less and less interest in his partner, it usually triggers a sense of insecurity and imbalance in the woman. These strong feelings may actually lead to a spontaneous burst in her libido to ensure her position as the only female in his life.

Let's Put It All Together

A relationship has a circular dynamic. Everything each spouse says or does or each individual reaction is what causes or determines the next level of interaction.

On a related note, I have been surprised to learn that men have an extremely difficult time understanding and accepting that most women have a lower sex drive than they do, that a lower drive does not have anything to do with them personally, and that there isn't anything medically wrong with their women. In their defense, I could see how their confusion could have been influenced by the following:

1. For centuries, women have been socialized to take care of their men's needs and show enthusiasm and excitement while doing it. As women have become more emancipated, less dependent on their men, and more focused on education, career, friends, hobbies, they have become less concerned with pleasing their men and have less energy to dedicate to their spouses. All of a sudden, messages that have been traditionally passed on from generation to generation are not re-enacted any longer. The women are changing the rules and feel just fine with doing so.

2. Most women in the **Lust Stage** of the relationship are highly sexual. They enjoy sex, they are very passionate, and they give men the message that they like sex as much as they do. The truth is that most women <u>really</u> enjoy sex as much as the men do during that phase, due to hormones and neurotransmitters. However, their biology changes as they become more secure in the relationship, while a man's biology doesn't. It's a <u>very normal</u> change that is not often discussed because most marriages may not take place. Men may not sign up for marriage just for the friendship without the sex. Thus, when the changes do take place, most men feel either duped or think about the next logical expla-

nation, which is that their spouses don't love them anymore.

3. Women sometimes use sex to get what they want in a relationship or to express their anger or payback toward their spouse. Of course, this "How to manage your man" technique has been taught to women from generation to generation so it is deeply ingrained in our brains to use our sexuality to get what we want especially, because it works. It has been an effective method of control for centuries. Yet, if you really think about it, it mostly has something to do with the fact that women don't need sex as much as men do. If women really had that high of a need for sex, they wouldn't sacrifice it so easily or give it up that often.

In the end, human relationships and sexuality are complicated and often difficult to understand. At any moment in time, the human sex drive could be influenced by tens of social, emotional, and cognitive, in addition to physical and medical, factors.

Nonetheless, what I've learned, time and time again, is that no matter what the reason, after lengthy sexual deprivation, both spouses become <u>highly sensitive and insecure</u> about themselves and the status of their relationship.

I have found that when there is no sex for an extended period of time, the explicit or implicit message communicated in the marriage sounds something like this:

> *"I want you to marry me, be ready and willing to give me sex when I, the low-sex-drive spouse, want it. However, I don't really need to have it that often any more. Most likely, this won't change much, so we won't be having sex more than once every couple of months, and I want you to be okay with that. Finally, I do not want you to ever look at other people, fantasize about other people, or cheat on me."*

Can you see how this could easily make someone feel trapped in a loveless marriage and consider it a breach of contract, and how, in time, it would lead to divorce?

As I listened to many similar stories, I always felt the spouses' sadness triggered by the fact that they ultimately feel helpless and hopeless. They both may feel as if there is something wrong with their relationship, with their partner, or with themselves. In most cases, this could not be any further from the truth.

As I explained in the previous chapter, this dynamic could be blamed on biology, or habituation, or it could simply be the typical course of a committed relationship.

The saddest part is that partners are usually not aware that this is normal; they don't want to acknowledge it as normal, and they don't talk about it. Instead of humorously accepting that their relationship is maturing, they may nag each other about it, but they often don't discuss the common reasons behind not being interested in sex.

They don't do it because they are ashamed, embarrassed, afraid of hurting the other one's feelings, or afraid of what it says about them if they are not interested. Over time, both partners may feel widely invalidated, misunderstood, estranged from each other, ashamed, or afraid that something is wrong with them.

This vicious downward spiral will continue with poor or limited communication, anger, lack of co-operation, and a high level of tension. Overall, it is a very sensitive subject for both people. Learning how to talk about it in a confident but empathic manner makes a whole world worth of difference. It is the key between making or breaking the relationship. That's why Chapter 6, on communication, is one of the most important chapters in this book.

Before we get there, however, I feel as if I wouldn't be doing my job if I didn't cover a few other areas that need to be considered. This book offers a quick behavioral solution that is a great patch for rough times. It is a great way to keep you together and engaged in the relationship while you work out through any other normal challenges that may arise in your relationship. But I do want to briefly mention a few other issues that affect sexuality and address possible venues of support.

Drugs and Therapy

On that note, getting a physical is always a good first line of defense because there are indeed many physical conditions or medications that affect sexuality. We always want to rule out physical problems, such as chronic heart, liver, or kidney conditions, diabetes, arthritis, anemia, menopause, chronic pain, physical disability, the side effects of chemotherapy, and side effects from medications such as antidepressants, antihypertensives, antihistamines, tranquilizers, and birth control pills. In addition, alcohol, tobacco, marijuana, cocaine, and opiates can also affect sexual performance.

If these are not factors that have led up to your changes, individual or couples' therapy is always an option. Many types of therapy are usually available. Some explore feelings, others focus on thoughts, and yet others focus on behaviors. Some are more integrative and try to combine all of these areas. Some focus on family history and relationships with previous caretakers that are being re-enacted in the current relationship. Certain types of therapy focus on unresolved issues or traumatic experiences.

In my opinion (although I am biased), any type of therapy (with a good therapist) is an opportunity for learning, self-awareness, or self-improvement. In addition, therapy can also address possible psychological causes of low sex-drive, such as depression, anxiety, sexual, physical, or emotional abuse, grief, stress, low self-esteem, and a poor body image. Unfortunately, therapy is often perceived as costly, time-consuming, and even embarrassing, so most individuals will not even consider therapy as a viable option. Most people will use books, online resources, or just the shoulder of a good friend.

This is one reason I wrote this book. I wanted to use all of my experience and education and put it in a book that people who are too embarrassed by counseling or can't afford therapy can use right away, before things get worse or before it's too late. The great news is that with only a few small changes, you can make a big difference in your relationship. The exciting thing about this method is that not only can it stop the relationship from its downward spiral but it can re-set it on a course of higher intimacy and connection. It can take you to Stage Four, otherwise called "Honest Love." Let me explain.

Honest Love

I think we have established by now that all relationships change over time. Most changes are healthy and normal, but I believe most people don't really know this and don't expect it. Most people expect the "fairy tale." And when the illusion of the fairy tale falls apart, most people are threatened by these changes in their relationship.

They are first scared by <u>conflict</u>. There is a sense that expressing disagreement means something is wrong with the relationship. They are also scared by the <u>loss of excitement</u> in their relationship. Not feeling the butterflies when they see each other may signify that they are falling out of love; it may mean the end of the relationship. Finally, they are scared of <u>being truthful</u> because the truth may hurt the partner's feelings.

Honest Love is understanding all of these phases of a relationship, predicting change, talking openly about it, and laughing about it together. Did I say talking openly about it? I mean truly wanting to know how these changes are affecting you, your partner, and your daily interactions.

All people who have been in a long-term relationship will say they don't always like their partners, and they don't always have loving feelings toward them, either. In fact, loving a spouse in the absence of hormonal desire is real love because it requires effort. I am not saying that loving your spouse should be treated as a chore, but I am saying that loving your spouse requires purposeful action if you want the relationship to last.

Honest Love is a mature relationship, grounded in both people understanding each other; it is focused on individual growth, team growth, and on appreciating shared interests along with your differences. In order to reach this level:

- Embrace your differences.

- Learn how to be honest in a gentle manner.

- Keep a sense of humor about your small, quirky differences; most of the small differences, although seemingly huge in the heat of the argument, will not be remembered in five years.

- Reconcile your big differences by talking, negotiating, and looking at pros and cons.

- Don't stop talking to each other.

- Don't stop having sex; it doesn't have to be hot or exciting, it just has to exist.

All of this does take some time and work, but, more important, it takes a strong willingness to compromise and accommodate each other's needs without losing yourself. The good news is that this book will show you how to achieve at least some of these milestones.

The Insight Corner

Have an honest discussion about the current stage of your relationship. How has intimacy changed for one of you? What are the positives? What are the negatives?

_____

_____

_____

_____

_____

4
The Big Reveal

Fred: *Hey, baby! I see you've had a rough day at the office. Why don't you and I go back to the bedroom, and I'll help you unwind?*

Susan: *Are you kidding? The kids have homework, we've got to eat, I need to give the kids a bath, and, honestly, I would like to catch up on "The Gossip Girl." But, can you finish in two minutes while the kids play Mario?*

Fred: *I am a Can-Do Guy! Two minutes is better than none.*

One of the myths of sex is that sex is always related to love, romance, and emotions. Well, the number of one-night stands and physical affairs that both men and women have had over time should be some proof that sex is also about hormones, animalistic desire, and sometimes, it is simply about "getting off."

This is very much like eating or sleeping. When you have it, you can think of other more important things like flowers, poems, and romance. Yet for those people who don't have it and who want it, sex becomes a necessity or a matter of survival. It becomes an <u>intrusive obsession</u>.

Yet what's the solution when we don't <u>feel</u> like having sex? Take one woman's raw disclosure: "*I just flat out don't want to be touched. I am tired, my senses are shut down, and I feel like he is in my space.*"

How do we get past that? Well, the good news is that with a very small change, you can make a huge difference in your relationship.

Generally speaking, most therapy (and almost every self-help book) insists on analyzing and changing your thoughts and feelings about sex before you get to see any progress in the bedroom.

Having reached a rut point in my marriage, I thought I should try something different. I thought, "Let's go with the behavior first, and see what happens." So, during one of those moments when my husband was nagging me for sex, I jokingly said, "Yes, but can you get it done in two minutes because I have other things I need to do?" He said "yes" and that's how *the 2-minute solution* was born.

Surprisingly, I have found that changing your sexual behavior and actions first may lead to different thoughts and feelings, which in turn may lead to even more sexual behavior.

It is true that most of us expect to change our feelings first before we take action. I am saying to do it the other way around. The only exception is if those feelings are of <u>disgust</u> or <u>pure resentment</u> toward your husband; these are indicators of bigger problems in the relationship. In this case, I highly recommend therapy first, to get to the bottom of those powerful feelings.

If this is not the case, though, don't wait for your feelings toward sex to change. It may be a very slow process or it may not happen; instead, just have sex. This is the basis for *the 2-minute solution.*

The 2-minute solution is something that should be added to your weekly routine, just like eating, showering, brushing your teeth, or exercising. It is simply having sex for two minutes when requested by either of the partners.

It is based on a mutual understanding that the sex will last only two minutes and there are no expectations of anything else. If it turns into a full session and both partners are honestly fully on board, then by all means the rules can be changed. But if one partner is willing and only able to spare two minutes, then both spouses should stick to that.

No Guilting, No Whining, No Complaining!

This is not "wearing your black lace, hanging off a chandelier, rocking your partner's world" kind of sex. It is "getting your partner off the fastest way possible" sex.

This does not have anything to do with performance, yours or your partner's.

This has nothing to do with expectations, because there are no expectations, other than getting sexual relief for the partner who absolutely needs it.

Although this can be perceived as primarily for the guy's immediate benefit, it is not always the case. In situations where the woman has a higher sex drive, having intercourse for two minutes and finishing it with manual stimulation can achieve the same goal: biological release.

Yes, I can hear some skeptical laughs from both men and women, but bear with me BECAUSE THIS WORKS! The idea behind this simple but effective concept is that it eliminates the biggest excuses:

- • "I don't have time."

- • "I am too tired."

- • "I am not in the mood."

- • "I have a headache."

- • "I have too many other things to do."

It Only Takes Two Minutes!

Okay, I may be stretching the truth a tiny bit. Obviously, two minutes is a play on words, because most guys would not be able to ejaculate that fast every time. So when I say two minutes, it may turn into five minutes but not more than that. And overall, it should not take more than ten minutes, if you do it twice a week (which is preferred for best results).

Here is a different way to think about it. We spend approximately:

- 35 minutes per week brushing our teeth

- • 140 minutes per week showering

- • 70 minutes shaving
- • 70 minutes combing our hair
- • 70 minutes putting on makeup
- • 360 minutes cleaning our house

It is hard to believe that a couple cannot find five to ten minutes in a week to have sex. There should be no reason why partners who truly care about each other and are willing to accommodate each other's needs should not be able to do this!

As far as the dialogue goes, the introductory scenario is a perfect example of how to introduce the idea to the other spouse. With time, as you get more comfortable, you should use as much romantic and playful banter as possible. However, there should not be any more inquisitive comments, lies, accusations, or trying to make the other person feel guilty.

This could happen just a couple of times per week and could make both spouses perfectly content. Not only can you achieve this without lying, hurting each other's feelings, or rejecting each other, it will actually improve the level of communication, and it will deepen the bond and the level of emotional intimacy.

Does it sound simple enough? Well, it is. It is a very low-maintenance technique. All you need is a good lubricant (KY Jelly or saliva), a timer, a willingness to change, an open mind, and a great sense of humor. For beginners, the mental mind-set may be a bigger challenge because you will have to let go of all preconceived ideas about sex, romance, roles, and expectations. You are starting with a clean slate.

This is important for both spouses: for the one with lower desire, as well as the one with higher desire. It is important for the high-desire spouse to understand that the 2-minute solution should <u>absolutely not be used</u> as a "bait and switch" diversion. It does not mean "Now that I am in, I am going to take twenty minutes and turn this into a love making session." This could happen, but let the low-desire partner decide that. If it doesn't happen, let it go. Don't pressure your spouse, and definitely don't make your spouse feel guilty.

The other important detail is that the low-desire spouse needs to start initiating and offering the two-minute sessions and not wait for the high-desire spouse to come begging. This will shift the gridlock that I described earlier.

"What do you do with the feeling of dread? If I have to do anything I don't like three times per week, it would lead me to dislike my day, be grumpy and resentful. How do I suppress the feeling?"

If it is such a strong feeling, don't do it three times a week. Start with once a week. Don't plan it; just find a day when you are in a good mood, and not very tired, and the relationship is in a good place. You'll be more willing to be generous. Focus on something your husband did well that day, ignore any other negative things you may tend to think about him, and just randomly offer him two minutes of sex. See what happens. Remember: no expectations, just go with the flow!

Finally, the communication dynamic will have to change. Both spouses will have to be honest about what they like or don't like, but it is primarily important for the low-desire spouse to be clear and outspoken. No more lame excuses or empty promises. He or she has to be completely honest. If the answer is "NOT RIGHT NOW," there should be a concrete alternative and follow-through as promised. The high-desire spouse has to accept it without pressure, sarcastic comments, eye rolling, and so on. Here are a few options:

- "Right now, I can only do two minutes. Are you okay with that?"

- "I am really not in the mood right now, but I can do two minutes before we go to bed tonight."

- "I am okay with taking a little longer until you finish, but please do it as fast as possible."

- "I would like to enjoy this a little longer and have fun with it, and see where it goes."

- "I am not in the mood for a long session. You can come first, but I want my turn also. Can we make it quick, though?"

These are indeed not passionate or romantic comments. They are very direct and to the point, but if you don't read too much into it and are just able to do it, you will start seeing the benefits shortly.

It is true, however, that it may take a little bit of time to get your man to accept that "two minutes" means just that. Interestingly enough, in my clinical practice, I have found that men had a more difficult time accepting this concept than women. It really throws men off. Although, in theory, men think and fantasize about quick sex and having sex all the time, they seem to have a tough time accepting that their wives or girlfriends are not interested in making love for an hour, three to five times per week.

In all fairness, the man may be confused because that was not the case during Stages One and Two, when you enjoyed having sex as much as he did. He may think of it as pity sex, just "throw him a bone" kind of sex.

**This is not pity sex.
It's just sex that should happen very fast!**

In addition, he may be concerned that he is not able to ejaculate that fast. This is a valid concern, and the truth is that sometimes he may be able to come that fast, and other times he won't. The idea is that as long as he truly does focus on ejaculating as fast as possible and not dragging it on for hours, it won't make a difference if it is two, three, or five minutes. Most women will hang in there for as long as needed, as long as they know you are doing your best to finish as soon as possible.

Hopefully, once a man can get mentally used to the idea of two minutes, especially when offered by the woman, he will be able to get over it and just ride the wave without over-thinking this whole process.

It is important to understand that *the 2-minute solution* is just one activity. We cannot rely on this activity alone to help us stay connected. This is just a solution that helps us bridge gender differences in sexual desire or helps us through stressful and busy times.

Yet intimacy comes in different flavors. That pretty much means a couple can do a lot of variations to feel emotionally and physically satisfied. For example, although men are generally said to want physical intercourse, while women prefer cuddling while watching a movie, the truth is that both men and women will experience different wants and needs at different moments in time, depending on what is going on in their lives.

I broke them down in three categories.

1. Purely emotional connection: calling each other, texting, emailing, writing notes to say "I love you," "I am thinking about you," "I miss you," or sexual innuendos while talking or texting.

2. Purely physical connection: brushing against each other, hugging, kissing, patting on the butt, massages, two-minute intercourse.

3. Emotional and physical connection: working out together, making out, trying new positions, the full combo of dinner, movie, and sex.

My first big point here is that for a successful relationship, every day, spouses should engage in at least one of these activities, no matter how small or how little time it takes.

My second big point is that when we date, we are used to doing things in a linear progression, all in one day: foreplay, intercourse, orgasm, and cuddling. When you are married, you need to move away from these expectations. You can have foreplay on one day, intercourse on another day, orgasm on a different day, and you can cuddle on the couch on a completely different day. For example:

Monday:	A relaxing massage in the hot tub (foreplay).
Tuesday:	Two minutes of intercourse, focus on the high-desire spouse.
Thursday:	Two minutes for the high-desire spouse and manual stimulation for the low-desire spouse.
Friday:	Cuddling on the couch while watching a movie.

Saturday	Two minutes of focus on the high-desire spouse.
Sunday:	Walking in the park or working out together.

In her book *The Sex-Starved Marriage*, Michele Weiner Davis (2003) quotes one husband: "If my wife initiated other forms of affection-a kiss for no reason, lingering about when hugging, a look, a smile, or even a knowing smirk-it would take the focus off the lack of making love because those forms of intimacy are even more important than sex sometimes."

As long as partners keep engaged, and honest, and are willing to accommodate each other, a couple can successfully negotiate and bridge the gap caused by gender differences or any discrepancies in the desire levels. And, as you will see in the next chapter, this comes with a few other perks and benefits for all parties involved.

The Insight Corner

This is an easy one. Try the 2-minute solution. How does it feel for you? How does it feel for your spouse? Talk about it.

_____

_____

_____

_____

5
More Reasons to Try the 2-Minute Solution

Have I persuaded you to take a chance and try the *2-minute solution*? I really hope so, but just in case you need an extra boost, here are a few more reasons.

Relationship Benefits

Obviously, this is the big one. If physical intimacy has been missing in your relationship and the lack of sex has affected your partner's psyche or yours, then *the 2- minute solution* is a great circuit breaker for a vicious, unhealthy cycle.

For best results, I recommend that this exercise be done two to three times a week for one entire month, but most people have reported a significant change in their attitude, as well as their partners' after one week.

Many report less irritability, with each other or the kids, more patience, more willingness to help around the house, more laughter, and more interest in being an active member of the family. All of this will lead to a boost in sexual energy, and it will increase the level of attraction between partners.

If you feel overwhelmed by the idea of having sex with such frequency, then don't do it that often. Just try it once a week to begin with. If it works for you to do it more often, that's great. If you are willing to do it only once a week, then do just that. It is still significantly better than nothing.

Practical Benefits

One of my economics professors in college once said that marriage is like a business venture. At that time, I thought this was one of the most unromantic and pessimistic things one could say about marriage. Today, fourteen years into my marriage, all I can say is, "Boy, was he right!" Dr. Helen Fisher also concurs with that statement, because she says that the reason for "Attached Love" (Stage 3) is to tolerate each other long enough to raise children until maturity.

I do have to agree that "tolerate" is a harsh word. I really do believe that marriage can be a communion where two people can enjoy each other's company, set and meet financial and personal goals together, enjoy hobbies and vacations together, and support each other through the tough times that life throws their way.

Nevertheless, I guarantee that all of this is impossible without sex and long-term physical intimacy. Consider *the 2-minute solution* the salt and pepper of your relationship, while all of the other crazy, hot bedroom moves can be the extra flavorful spices, such as oregano, basil, and thyme. I am sure you get the point.

Physical Benefits

Although the core of this book is based on bridging the gap in the sex drive between men and women and hence the tone of "think about your husband," the truth is that sex in itself is not just for pleasure. According to a significant amount of research, it has a tremendous positive effect on your health. Here is a quick summary of why you should be having sex for you and not just for your husband (Robinson & Smith, 2014):

1. *Strengthens your immune system*. People who have sex have higher levels of an antibody called immunoglobulin A (IgA), which defends your body against germs, viruses, and other intruders.

2. *Eases stress.* Touching and hugging can release your body's natural feel-good hormones, endorphins and oxytocin. These rev up your brain's pleasure and reward system and in turn help ward off anxiety and depression.

3. *Improves sleep.* After orgasm, the hormone prolactin is released, which is responsible for feelings of relaxation and sleepiness.

4. *Improves bladder control*. A strong pelvic floor is important for avoiding incontinence, something that will affect about 30 percent of women at some point in their lives, especially those who had children.

5. ***Lowers heart attack risk.*** A good sex life benefits your heart. Besides being a great way to raise your heart rate, sex helps keep your estrogen and testosterone levels in balance.

6. ***Lessens pain.*** Vaginal stimulation can block chronic back and leg pain, and many women have told us that genital self-stimulation can reduce menstrual cramps, arthritic pain, and, in some cases, even headache. Again, the endorphins that are released during an orgasm closely resemble morphine, and they effectively relieve pain.

7. ***Causes lighter periods (with fewer cramps).*** When a woman orgasms, the increased number of uterine contractions can also help expel blood and tissue more quickly, helping to end her period faster. Having sex while menstruating (as unappealing as it sounds) has also been shown to help decrease the risk for endometriosis (a common condition in which uterine tissue grows outside of the uterus, causing pelvic pain and sex that hurts).

The Insight Corner

What is better for your health? Exercising fifteen minutes, three times per week, or exercising for one hour, once per month?

What is better for your marriage? Having two-minute sex sessions, three times per week, or a thirty-minute sex session once per month?

6
What Is Your
Communication Style?

As I mentioned earlier, sex and communication go hand-in-hand in a marriage. Good-quality communication is the essence of a strong relationship. It doesn't matter what the disagreements or differences are, being able to speak to each other in a caring, respectful, and empathic way will help ride you out the inevitable waves of a marriage. Of course, communication about sex (or the lack of it) is equally important. All of the likes and dislikes, do's and don'ts, have their place in making a relationship better.

Unfortunately, "most couples enter marriage with impossible dreams and unrealistic expectations. Marriage is essentially a partnership and an occupation. If people wrote out job descriptions, fully listing exactly what they wished to give and get from marriage, and if each potential partner studied the other's lists before getting engaged, much grief and many dashed hopes could be averted" (Lazarus, 2001).

As a matter of fact, communication, in general, is not a strength for most couples. Communication is not a skill that we are born with. It is a skill we learn. We learn it from our caregivers, first and foremost, then from our teachers, our friends, our co-workers, and our managers. As a matter of fact, every person we have ever talked to has potentially affected our communication style. Those who had great role models in the art of conversation will manage this process very well. It is also a process that extends to work, to our home, or to the bedroom, because our style is usually consistent across all areas of our lives.

In my experience with couples' therapy, communication is critical to the survival of the relationship, but it can be also very difficult to do successfully. Although many aspire toward intimacy, spouses are often afraid to open up and share their true feelings and thoughts. Most people start like that during the dating phase or during the honeymoon; however, as the relationship continues, true personalities, preferences, and styles of communication ultimately reveal themselves. And soon, they share what they think the other one wants to hear or what will be met with the least amount of resistance, otherwise called the "yes, dear-syndrome."

In terms of communication styles, most people will find themselves in what therapists refer to as "passive," "aggressive," or "passive-aggressive" modes of communicating their emotions, their thoughts, and, last but not least, their sexual preferences and desires. In this chapter, I will briefly review these communication patterns, how to avoid or overcome barriers to effective communication, and will offer some solutions for improvement. These styles are usually part of one's personality and are displayed with family, friends, co-workers, and of course, significant others. Communication styles apply particularly in personal relationships and affect a couple's dynamic on a day-to-day basis in all sorts of matters, including intimacy. In addition, because this book revolves around the off-limits topic of sex, I will apply some of these concepts to typical marital conversations about sex.

Communication Quiz

First, let's do a brief personal assessment quiz to identify your style of communication:

Depending on your choice, write A, B, C, or D after each question. After answering all of the questions, refer to the Score Interpretation Key at the end of the quiz.

1. **You are tired from work, barely have any energy to make dinner, and your husband is asking for sex. What do you do?**

   A. You think about how you are tired of giving every ounce of energy to others but don't want to upset him, so you say, "Yes."

   B. You respond, "Are you freaking kidding me? Is sex all you think about?"

   C. You have sex and then shut down and do not talk to him for the rest of the night.

   D. You say, "I am sorry honey. I am *so* not in the mood tonight, but tomorrow will be perfect" (and you actually keep your promise).

2. You are in the middle of watching your favorite show when your spouse comes in and asks for a favor that may take thirty minutes. You would:

A. Stop watching your show and go help him.

B. Say, "No" and keep watching your show.

C. Go help him but then interrupt all of his shows for the rest of the week.

D. Ask him to wait until your show is over and help then.

3. You are in the middle of sex and your husband is taking a lot longer than you are up for.

A. You lie there until he is finished and don't say anything.

B. You say, "Are you done yet? I am bored out of my mind."

C. You lie there until he is done but then make excuses for the rest of the month about why you can't have sex.

D. You ask, "Honey, is there anything I can do to help you finish a little faster tonight?"

4. You think that your spouse may be cheating on you. You don't have a lot of proof except some slight indicators that something is off. What do you do?

A. You think, "This really bothers me, but I am afraid that if I speak up, I will only push him further away."

B. You assume he is cheating and attack him, without giving him a chance to explain.

C. You don't say anything because you don't want to make waves, but you start avoiding him: no sex, no kissing, barely any talking, just the minimum necessary to make it as roommates.

D. You sit down with him, discuss the information you have, give him a chance to explain, and then make a decision on how to proceed further.

5. **Your spouse tells you he loves you very much, but that the extra weight you have gained from your pregnancy five years ago bothers him.**

A. You don't say anything, become really depressed, and don't do anything about your diet.

B. You say, "You are so shallow and selfish. I had your kid. Just deal with it. You either like me the way I am, or don't let the door hit you on your way out."

C. You tell him he is right and you'll work on it, but then you turn around, call your girlfriend and complain about it without any intention of changing.

D. You admit to him and to yourself that hearing this makes you feel sad and uncomfortable and that you will need some time to process the conversation. At a later time, you agree to make healthy changes to your diet and ask him to join the gym with you.

6. You feel as if your spouse has been harboring a grudge against you, but you don't know why. You would:

A. Pretend you are unaware of his anger and ignore it, hoping it will go away on its own.

B. Rev up your anger, trying to get a step ahead of him, and forcefully tell him: "You can't be angry with me. I *am* angry with *you.*"

C. Not say anything but start picking unrelated fights until one of you blows up.

D. You say, "Honey, I feel there is tension between us. Are you mad at me or at something else? Can we please talk about it?"

7. You don't believe in spanking your children. Your spouse doesn't really agree, but he'll go along most of the time until he loses his temper. You would:

A. Let it go; it doesn't happen too often.

B. Start yelling at him in front of the kids that he should not spank them

C. Don't say anything, but you find yourself taking the kids' side and punishing the father for the rest of the week.

D. Ask your husband to meet you in a different room, where you express your disagreement with spanking and offer him an alternative.

8. Your mother-in-law tells you she is coming over to stay with you for a month. Your husband doesn't say much about it, but you believe a month is too long. What would you do?

    A. You really dislike the idea but decide not to say or do anything about it.

    B. Take your frustration out on your husband, saying, "Is your mother out of her mind? How rude can she be? I don't really want her here at all."

    C. You don't say anything, but when she gets here you do everything you can to make her visit uncomfortable, hoping that she will leave early.

    D. You talk it out with your husband and to see whether you can both come up with a shorter alternative and a way to communicate it back to her.

9. It's date night. Your husband was in charge of planning, but after a rough day at work, he totally forgot about it. What would you do?

    A. You don't say anything, but are unable to stop thinking about how he takes you for granted.

    B. You tell him, "Are you serious? So what if you had a rough day? I had a crappy day, too, but I didn't forget about it."

    C. You let it go, but next time you conveniently forget something he cares about just to make a point.

D. You say, "I am really sad about it and part of me feels like you don't care much about these date nights, but I do understand you had a bad day. I'll let you make it up to me this weekend."

10. You've been reading a sex book and decided you want more manual stimulation from your husband. You are okay with intercourse and you are okay with doing it for your husband but it's not your favorite. What would you do?

A. You can't do or say anything about it. You don't want to hurt his feelings.

B. You say, "I am really tired of you coming all the time and me not so much. From now on, no sex for you until I get what I want first."

C. You don't say anything but take his hand and show him what to do. If he doesn't do it long enough or often enough, you assume he just doesn't care about what you want, so you stop having sex.

D. You say, "Honey, I enjoy having intercourse, but I definitely enjoy it more when you use your hands. Can we do that more often? It makes my orgasms so much better!"

Score Interpretation Key

Mostly A's: You have a Passive Communication style

"Everyone else is okay, but I am not okay" is a typical thought of a passive communicator. This individual is naturally inclined or has developed a habit of avoiding expressing his or her feelings, thoughts, and opinions. The individual is afraid of speaking up or may believe he or she is not important enough or worth the attention. Passive communication is often a sign of low self-esteem and is often conducive of anxiety and depressive disorders.

Most of the time, passive individuals are focused on pleasing or accommodating others, and avoiding conflict; they would describe themselves as hypersensitive, but they ignore their feelings, cover them up, or rationalize that their feelings are not a big deal. In time, the unfulfilled grievances build up and cause these individuals to "blow up" in an extreme manner. Furthermore, they will likely feel extremely ashamed and guilty after such an explosive episode, and they will return to being passive. It is highly possible that these individuals grew up thinking that they would be punished for speaking the truth or voicing their opinions.

> **_Passive communicators:_**
> - Will listen well, but will fail to voice their thoughts and feelings.
> - Will often shut down.
> - Will speak softly.
> - Have poor eye contact.
> - Will often allow others to infringe on their rights.

Mostly B's: You have an Aggressive Communication style

> **_Aggressive communicators:_**
> - Blame others.
> - Use labels.
> - Criticize constantly.
> - Threaten and give ultimatums.
> - Nag and wear the opponent out.

"I am okay, you are not okay" is the motto of an aggressive communicator. This is the opposite extreme of the previous profile, the passive communicator. This means that this individual is naturally inclined or has learned to express his or her feelings, thoughts, and opinions in a very loud and hostile manner that often violates the rights of others. Despite frequently being misinterpreted as confidence, aggressive communication is actually a sign of low self-esteem and is often rooted in past physical or emotional abuse. This individual may view him- or herself as superior and entitled and uses accusatory statements and domineering language.

Mostly C's: You have a Passive-Aggressive Communication style

"You are not okay but I will let you believe you are at least in the beginning until I find a way to get back at you" is the motto of a passive-aggressive communicator. This is a hybrid style. This means that the individual will appear passive on the surface, but will sabotage or act out the anger or disapproval in a subtle and indirect manner. Messages will often sound unclear and confusing. The individual uses lies, sarcasm, teasing, ridiculing, false praise, and insinuations.

When in a relationship with a Passive-Aggressive (P-A) communicator, you may feel as if the P-A is playing games, as if the person doesn't mean what he or she says, that there is always something more and you have to guess it.

It's common for Passive-Aggressive people to leave clues around and wait to be caught in an affair, rather than tell the spouse directly that they are not happy in the relationship. Other examples are: when the woman picks a sexually charged situation to tell her husband she doesn't like having sex with him or the woman avoids sex altogether to force her husband to ask her questions about what's wrong, rather than speaking up about what bothers her.

Mostly D's: You have an Assertive Communication style

"I am okay, you are okay" is the motto of a confident or assertive communicator. This means that the individual is naturally and easily able to express his or her feelings, thoughts, and opinions.

This individual is able to firmly but respectfully promote his or her rights and needs without hurting the other's feelings or infringing on others' rights. Assertive communication is characterized by fairness and strength and it is the preferred and healthiest style. This style is often a sign of strong self-esteem.

What's This Got to Do with My Sex Life?

So, how does one's communication style relate to _the 2-minute solution_? _The 2-minute solution_ is all about assertiveness, and this is the main reason I included sex and communication in this book. It is about being able to <u>tell</u> the truth and being able to <u>hear</u> the truth. It is about clear and direct communication, because assertiveness occurs when the message is stated plainly and directly to your partner and it includes:

HONESTY about what you want;

EMPATHY toward what your partner wants;

LISTENING to your partner and VOICING your opinion;

and

COMPROMISE and finding a middle ground.

By now, you've probably figured out that assertive communication is the core of a healthy relationship, but, of course, like any other skill, assertive communication takes time and practice. Because most individuals <u>are not </u>natural assertive communicators, the next question is, how do you get there?

In the following chapter, we will review some basic steps to help you change your communication style and some tips on how to make practice of assertive communication in the bedroom a little less daunting.

The Insight Corner

What's your communication style? What is your spouse's? Are there any changes either of you would like to make in terms of communication?

_____

_____

_____

7

Tips and Tricks to Enhance Assertiveness in the Bedroom

For those of you who are ready to dive into it but need an extra confidence boost, here are a few steps to assist you in the bedroom:

1. Make the decision to own your sexuality and communicate your sexual needs confidently. The first step in any change process is to want it and to become <u>very aware</u> of wanting to change. Once you are open to change, you'll be open to a lot of opportunities that you may have ignored in the past.

2. Inform your spouse of your decision and ask for his or her support and patience. Ask for your spouse's honest feedback about how you come across when you talk. This way, you'll be able to identify your communication style, with its strengths and weaknesses. Also, ask how your sexuality affects him or her. Apologize in advance for anything that may not be communicated in "the right way." Reassure each other about the commitment to make this better for both of you.

3. Explore your style. It's important to try to understand what led to your communication style. Is there anything in your childhood or

in the way you were brought up that kept you from speaking up? Also, find out whether you feel any ambivalence toward becoming more confident and speaking up about sex. For example, for a woman who has been faking orgasms, being honest and speaking up about what is truly pleasurable to her can be extremely scary. She may be afraid of hurting her husband's feelings, or taking responsibility for her sexuality, or may be worrying about whether she can actually have an orgasm. Each of these concerns could be a deterrent to change, but I urge you to push through. With a supportive husband, you can work through all of these concerns and experience extremely mutually satisfying results.

4. When is the best time to talk about sex with your spouse? Pick the right time and place. Generally speaking, don't talk about sexual problems in the bedroom, before bedtime, or if one of you has had a rough day. Also, pick your battles. If you are a passive communicator who has been bottling up a lot of stuff, don't bring it all up at once. It could be that sex takes too long, it hurts after a while, you don't feel that your spouse cares about what you want, you don't like oral sex, hand jobs take too long, and so on. It may be overwhelming for the other spouse to know you've been dissatisfied for so long. Pick one concern at a time and work through that one first. If you are an aggressive communicator who is now trying to change, don't shut down on everything. Take your time, pick the areas

you want to work on, and turn down the intensity of the comments.

5. Sound it out in your head first before you say it. A little planning can avoid explosive conversations. Imagine that your spouse is saying this to you. How would you feel? Is there a better way to phrase it? Take a time-out if the conversation is getting heated or going in the wrong direction. Don't be offensive. Have a keyword that signifies a "below the belt, unfair" comment. Come back and solve the problem when everyone is in a better place.

6. Get a couple of sex books or sex board games. Sometimes it's difficult to start talking about sex when you haven't done it in a long time. It's awkward and embarrassing. You can use the books or the games as a prompt. Pick random topics and talk about them. Start with fairly neutral topics before you dive into the emotionally charged ones.

7. Finally, practice, practice, practice. It is very important to remember that both spouses have pitfalls in their communication process. It is rare that a couple is made up of an assertive communicator and a communicator in one of the other categories. My point is that both spouses will have some work to do. I really can't stress enough that communication is one of those skills that requires practice for improvement. You cannot become a better communicator by reading about it. You become a better communicator by communicating!

These, of course, are the Cliff Notes on how to improve your communication. Reading up on the subject is the best way to get going, but practicing what you read is what really makes a difference. Having a supporting spouse who is willing to practice with you will make it that much better. I truly believe that a caring spouse is the best practice partner, because he or she is willing to hang in there and forgive your mistakes, hopefully, just as much as you are willing to hang in there and forgive your spouse's.

Because, believe me, you both will make mistakes. You both will say the wrong things at the wrong time in the wrong tone of voice and with the wrong demeanor.

Learning how to communicate better in a relationship is a very emotional process and it is often very draining, which is why I frequently have to encourage people not to give up.

In the beginning, changing your communication style looks like a pendulum. On one hand, passive people will likely sound aggressive the first few times they try to express themselves. On the other hand, aggressive people will likely shut down and become passive in an effort not to be too aggressive and offend their spouses. Unfortunately, that throws off the partner, which will in turn provoke an overreaction on their part, and that will cause the first partner to go back to his or her original communication style, which in turn will make both partners think they cannot change.

You become a better communicator by communicating

So, an essential part of this process is the partner's reaction to the change. It's like the other half of a very important mathematical equation. The partner will need to remember what is going on, that this is "role-playing" or a "training exercise". He or she should breathe, remain calm, and continue to be understanding.

A very easy trick to start your practice with is one that therapy manuals and therapists love. It's called the "I" statements. This is the simple formula that allows you to express your feelings:

1. Describe what triggered your thoughts or feelings.

2. Describe the thoughts or feelings.

3. Provide a simple explanation.

4. Make a request, stating what you need, and stand by it.

For example:

"When you ignore me, I feel as you don't care about me. I feel that I am being taken for granted. I would like it if you at least acknowledged me."

"I know you may think I am blaming you. I really am not. It is difficult for me to talk about this subject, so can you please do your best to listen without thinking I am attacking you?"

Yes, even with assertive communication, feelings WILL still get hurt. Focusing on hurt feelings will often push one person into a defensive mode, which could result in his or her shutting down or in an aggressive response. Either way, the conversation is over. After a while, too many conversations cut too short will result in both partners feeling misunderstood, and uncared for, and ultimately will lead to their growing apart.

Conversely, pushing through the hurt feelings and continuing the conversation, listening to each other, and trying to see the other's point of view, just as with the physical pain at the gym, will often result in a higher level of emotional intimacy, and immense growth in the relationship.

Eight Rules of Verbal and Nonverbal Communication for the 2-Minute Solution

This next section is something I use and refer to in every couples' therapy session when I introduce *the 2-minute solution*. It is a compilation of tips and tricks that will enhance the experience:

1. Say what you mean and mean what you say.

2. Express what you want, rather than what you don't want.

3. Focus on the present, here-and-now feelings and behaviors. Be in the moment. It's only two to five minutes. Don't let your mind wander. Focus on your sensations and tell your partner what feels good.

4. Be open to giving feedback to your spouse. Identify specifics: "Touch me here. Slower. Faster." Take his hand and guide him through the process.

5. Be gentle when you communicate. Be aware of nonverbal messages. No eye rolling, no puffing, no lying there like a dead fish. Don't make it so obvious that you don't like it. This won't make it go faster and it is offensive. If it is uncomfortable, gently ask to change positions or give different specific instructions.

6. Instead, heavy breathing, moaning, licking of the lips, or touching your breasts may speed up the process, if you are so inclined. Be as active as you can for two to five minutes. Although it may feel a little fake, "fake it till you make it" sometimes tricks your brain into feeling sexier, which in turn may lead to a more enjoyable experience.

7. No checking your phone, Facebook, or Twitter account during sex or during a conversation about sex. I never thought I would have to add this one, but apparently it's a growing problem.

8. Use humor. I can't stress this enough. Sex is funny, especially in a marriage. We all tend to take sex too seriously. Especially when sex feels like a chore, turn that around and make it funny. You can always diffuse the tension with a good laugh.

This process takes time, effort, and a lot of emotional energy. As you embark on this journey to change the communication dynamic in your relationship, there will be many frustrating times when you feel as if you do not get each other, and you are not on the same page or, sometimes, not even in the same book.

As you hit those tough moments, I can anticipate that you will not want to be intimate and have sex for a while. However, **my rule of thumb is: don't starve your relationship for sex for more than two to three weeks.**

I also know that we like to talk about makeup sex and how it makes the fight (or the argument) better. Once again, this may be the case for a new couple. In a long-term relationship, where fights, arguments, and annoyances with each other happen on a weekly basis, spouses have a tendency to keep track of points scored, rather than think of makeup sex.

Thus, it is hard for the person whose feelings just got hurt in yet another argument to want to have sex. It would be like losing another fight; it's like helping the other side win again. Therefore, sex is the last thing on this person's mind.

Although it's a natural tendency, keeping track of points is the WORST thing to do in a marriage. Don't get me wrong: we all do it, but it is still the worst thing to do. When you keep track of points, you are on different teams. It's a competition, not a partnership. In a competition, the only goal is to crush your opponent. This is a win-lose proposition in a relationship. This will end the relationship.

The goal of *the 2-minute solution* is to help reset any argument, fight, rivalry, or rut that has occurred between you and your spouse. Use sex not as a punishment but as an attempt for both of you to reinforce your partnership.

So, with that said, keep having sex and don't give up on talking. The sex may not be great, but it will keep the hormones at a manageable level, will allow your clear brains to do adequate talking, and will help both of you to maintain hope that everything and anything can be worked through.

Positive Phrases That Demonstrate Reassurance and Appreciation

Generally speaking, we don't do enough of this: not in our intimate relationships and not in our relationships with our children, our coworkers, or with ourselves. Human nature has a tendency to focus on the negative, primarily because we want to fix what is wrong, but we often don't stop to acknowledge what is right.

I will take you on a little detour to reinforce this point. One of my favorite stories is the Native-American tale of the two wolves: "One evening an old Cherokee told his grandson about a battle that goes on inside people.

He said, "My son, the battle is between two wolves inside us all. One is <u>Evil</u> - It is anger, envy, jealousy, sorrow, regret, greed, arrogance, self-pity, guilt, resentment, inferiority, lies, false pride, superiority, and ego. The other is <u>Good</u> - It is joy, peace, love, hope, serenity, humility, kindness, benevolence, empathy, generosity, truth, compassion, and faith.

The grandson thought about it for a minute and then asked his grandfather: "Which wolf wins?" The old Cherokee simply replied, "The one you feed."

On that note, in any relationship, we can choose to focus on the positive traits of our partners or the negatives. While I am not suggesting to live in denial and to ignore your true feelings about anything that happens in your relationship, I have found a solid formula to measure a successful relationship: three positive interactions to one negative interaction. Any time the balance tips in the opposite direction, at least one of the partners is going to start having doubts about the strength or the worth of his or her relationship.

Thus, please focus on your partner's positive qualities for a day. See what a difference that makes. Acknowledge these qualities out loud. Do it throughout the day as well as in the bedroom. These positive reassurances are just the sprinkles on top of everything else you have learned so far. These are phrases that could refer to you as a couple or to your partner's efforts and accomplishments. The following phrases should serve as quick reminders about how much you still care for each other sexually, despite the fact that you may not show it as often as you did while dating.

1. "I know we'll handle this together."

2. "I am sure we can resolve this."

3. "Look at how much we have accomplished so far."

4. "You took a lot of time thinking things through."

5. "You are turning me on more than you realize."

6. "After all of this time, I still find you very attractive."

7. "I like the way you touched me."

8. "I like the way you say I love you, even when we are having a rough time."

9. "You look great."

10. "You look hot in that outfit." Or even a simple:

11. "I like your new haircut."

8

10 Random Things Married Women Want to Tell Their Husbands but Don't Always Dare To

Conversation in the boardroom of a pharmaceutical company:

Executive 1: *"Boys, our boner pill worked so well for men, we have decided to make one for women.*

Research staff: *But sir, the data shows that women naturally don't care that much about sex.*

Executive 1: *No, the data shows that four out of five women suffer from Sleepy Vagina Syndrome.*

Executive 2: *Absolutely brilliant! We can have a marketing campaign with a questionnaire:*

- *Are you tired and don't feel like having sex?*
- *Would you rather watch Channing Tatum than have sex with your husband?*
- *Are you a woman?*

Then you may have S.V.S. Ask your doctor about Vagiwake, the pink pill that will wake up your vagina and make you want to have sex with your husband every day."

My husband wrote this dialogue after he heard me ranting about how much I dislike the pharmaceutical and medical communities for trying to trick women into believing there is something wrong with them just because they don't want to have sex all the time.

In this chapter, I want to touch on ten random things about married women's sexuality that I strongly believe husbands should be aware of. I do have to agree that hearing these facts won't necessarily make men feel good, and some may be a shocker, but, armed with new communication techniques, I hope you can talk these out with your spouse. I also hope that once you get past the shock, you can make it fun and can laugh out together.

1. **Just because women are not interested in sex, does not mean there is something medically wrong with them.**

   The first one is related to the introductory dialogue. While the "Sleepy Vagina Syndrome" does not exist, it is true that in order to get funding for a "female Viagra," pharmaceutical companies had done a need analysis to find the necessary data to persuade the investors.

   Their research methodology was founded on a very generic "yes or no" questionnaire about female sexual difficulties. Some of the issues covered were: inability to climax, physical pain during sex, not finding sex pleasurable, anxiety during sex, and difficulty with lubrication to name a few.

Well, what do you think they found out? The results indicated that 80 percent of women suffer from any or all of these issues at one point or another in their lives. At that time, drug companies decided to define this epidemic and lump it under the umbrella of "female sexual disorders" and - voila, now 80 percent of women would benefit from medication of some sort. Of course, that in itself was enough for many people to pay attention.

However, the most idiotic thing about this is that if 80 percent of women share similar concerns, doesn't that become the norm? Doesn't that make it normal and healthy behavior? Aren't we just trying to medicate ordinary life?

For those interested in this topic, I highly recommend watching Liz Canner's documentary *Orgasm, Inc.* (available on Netflix) or reading the work of Dr. Leonore Tiefer, who has dedicated her last fifteen years to exposing the truth behind the drug industry's activities regarding women's sexuality.

I have never done a formal study, but for years I have heard married women say that sex is usually low on their to-do list. Their mental and physical energy covers work, kids, chores, friends, and family stuff, so when they finally have a minute, they usually prefer a book, a movie, a glass of wine, and a lot of sleep to recuperate. Sex is only occasionally on the list, and women are getting tired of apologizing about it or trying to pretend this is not the case.

I don't want to overwhelm you with too much scientific literature, but I did pick a few research studies to highlight the differences in sexual attitudes and desire between men and women:

- According to Laumann, Gagnon, Michael, and Michaels (1994), men think about sex more often than women. Over half of the men in their national sample reported thinking about sex every day, whereas only one-fifth of the women reported thinking about sex that often.

- Men report more frequent sexual desire than women: 91 percent of men and only 52 percent of women experienced sexual desire several times a week (Beck, Bozman, and Qualtrough, 1991).

- Julien, Bouchard, Gagnon, and Pomerleau (1992) found that husbands and wives agreed that the men were more sexually active and frisky. Even more relevant, Julien et al. (1992) found that men were more likely than women to report having less sex in marriage than they wanted.

2. Many women do like sexually explicit materials.

Yes, I know this statement may appear contradictory to my previous point, so I should rephrase it as "Physically, many women are turned on by sexually explicit materials and even porn." However, many women have a difficult time allowing themselves to go with what feels good physically, due to years and years of hearing that "all porn is gross, dirty, demeaning to women, and made only for men's pleasure." Of course, there is some truth in this statement, but it's not entirely true.

It is true that most women may not be interested in the hard-core porn that's targeting the male population but there are plenty of videos for women or books with arousing titles such as *Dangerous Seduction, Feel the Heat*, or *Wicked Pleasure*. These are all on the stands of Barnes and Noble and often feature a picture with some guy and his rock-hard abs on the cover. We may not like to admit it, but these books do constitute porn.

Actress Mindy Kaling humorously stated on Esquire.com: "Women love sex tapes. Not porn, but sex tapes because scandal is titillating; if you want to trick us into watching porn, tell us the girl in it is famous and we just haven't heard of her yet."

On a side note and closely related to the point I made above, is that the same pharmaceutical companies that spent millions on trying to sell their "magic pill" to improve women's sex drive conveniently forgot to mention one important "detail." In their research study, right before "popping their new pill," women had to watch soft porn. In reality, this, and not the medication, is the true factor that increased their sexual desire. Thus, the moral of the story is that women may benefit from watching a good quality soft-core porn (yes, there is such a thing) or reading a sexually explicit book, and this could be enough to jump-start their sex drive occasionally. Husbands just have to be around when that happens.

Now, some women are very open and will embrace this kind of suggestive material; all you have to do is find something that appeals to them. Others, however, may not be willing to try this. Often, religion, a conservative upbringing, and culture-specific messages may prevent them from such experimentation. Despite the fact that these movies or books may turn them on, some may feel too much guilt or a feeling of "being dirty or wrong," so they will just plainly refuse to do it.

Social learning may have something to do with it again. Historically speaking, men have been trained to listen to their bodies. So when they get an erection, it pretty much indicates that they are sexually primed and ready to go. And, from a physical perspective, that can happen a lot.

Yet women have been socialized to be quiet and caring, have good manners, control their urges, their anger, and their passion because it's not "ladylike." After hundreds of years of such conditioning, women often find it difficult to identify when they are physically turned on, and sometimes, when they do, they feel guilty about it. It is more difficult for women to distinguish between physical, emotional, or mental turn-ons. Because we were socially trained to follow our emotions or our minds, we don't always respond to when our bodies when they tell us we are ready for sex.

3. Married women like to fantasize about sex a lot more than actually have sex.

Many married women still crave the passion and the exhilaration of being sexually pursued, but this is frequently a mental and emotional craving. Physically, it is often difficult to re-experience the butterflies of a new relationship while in an old relationship. This is pretty standard stuff for both men and women. However, most women are not willing to give up a perfectly good relationship and threaten their kids' home for a hot moment with the pool boy; thus, they often engage in daydreaming or night fantasies about steamy and passionate affairs.

Women can create a script and a movie and can perfect it by running through the details over and over again. The fantasy usually includes a story of pursuit, and hot, inexplicable passion with a man of interest who looks amazing, says the right things at the right time, and touches her on the perfect spots, all in a perfect ambiance of her choice. Having sex in reality would often ruin the perfect relaxing movie, so why would we want to do that?

So, what's a guy to do? Well, don't get angry and don't fight it. Try to find out when those good dreams happen, and just be around, offering your services to finish off a job that's already been started.

4. Married women don't care about multiple orgasms. Time matters!

Seriously, what woman who is married, with kids, a household, a job, or all of these has time for multiple orgasms? Like, how many orgasms do you actually need? I think this is another example of the American "super-size" obsession, where everything is bigger, better, and faster, and happens more often. Now, I do strongly believe that all women, even if they don't have any interest in sex, could benefit from having one good orgasm. Yet, nothing is worse than a spouse putting pressure on himself or on the female to achieve orgasm, especially if it's done through intercourse. Sex can get a little boring if it involves being drilled or jackhammered for thirty minutes. It is definitely not as exciting as they make it look in porn!

5. Women's interest in sex is affected by their body image, as well as by looking at their man's body image.

Our body image affects us tremendously in bed and, although we shouldn't, we do constantly compare ourselves to other women. Take, for example, what we get on the cover of pretty much every magazine out there: a gorgeous woman, typically an airbrushed size 2, half naked, wearing black lace, and always available and extremely willing to satisfy. Women interpret these ever-present messages as a representation of the ideal woman in terms of looks, health, and sexuality. Because it is impossible for most women to meet this ideal, these messages lead to frustration, self-doubt, unhealthy thoughts of inadequacy, and lower self-esteem. This will surely affect a woman's view of herself and her sexuality, and, in turn, it will definitely affect her thoughts, feelings, and actions in the bedroom.

At the same time, we also have to get real. I will say something that may send shock waves, so brace yourself for it. Your appearance, as well as your spouse's appearance, will affect the way you feel about each other sexually. If, when you met, you were fifty pounds lighter, those fifty pounds will affect your relationship and the sexual dynamic. Yes, it sounds shallow to blame weight or a change in appearance for the change in our sex drive, but if you are trying to awaken that animalistic desire, sometimes fewer cheeseburgers will do the trick.

Although we may not like to admit it, we have shallow thoughts, just as men do; we are attracted to a six-pack a whole lot more than to a beer belly. Therefore, make it a goal for you and your spouse to get healthy together. Go on a diet together. Exercise together. Exercise will make you feel sexier. Physically fit men and women rate themselves as more sexually desirable, have more energy, and feel more confident and more attractive. The extra endorphins will often lead to more sex.

6. Trading sex for chores is not prostitution.

Women trade household chores for sex. I do mean with their husbands. Men: Don't be offended; just take advantage of the offer. Household chores - what a boring, tedious, exhausting waste of life this is - unless you are really angry or anxious, in which case cleaning your house is really therapeutic.

Although we've been moving in the equality direction and husbands are more involved nowadays than they were in the 1950s, the burden of getting these chores done or managing the process still falls primarily on women. And what a process this is: extremely energy depleting, not always rewarding, and definitely not sexy. A few months into a marriage, it is kind of fun because you are playing house. Ten years into it - not as much. Women want the help, need the help, and expect the help from their husbands. Some are more vocal about it; others are not.

No matter what, there is a strong relationship between the husband's participation in the household chores and the amount of sex happening in that house (Voydanoff and Donnelly, 1999). It's hard to decide which one comes first. It's kind of like the chicken and the egg. I don't know whether women first withhold sex because they are not happy with the husband's level of participation in the house or whether the lack of sex causes the husband not to participate, but research shows that there is a strong correlation. In their study, Elliott and Umbersom (2008) share some quotes from the participants:

"If I have had a really good day, and you have been helpful, I would say you took out the trash, and you brought the trashcans in, and you mowed the lawn and everything. Those are the things that work for me to kind of get me going."

Or,

"I think for guys, generally speaking, sex is always a priority. For women, it just depends because of wherever they are in their lives. I am more concerned about the bills, the kids, daily routines, things that needed to get done. Even dishes or laundry are a priority before any leisure time or sex."

We may not agree with these statements, we may not like the situation, or we may be in denial and say this is not happening to us, but honestly, this is characteristic of a lot of households, so why not take advantage of it and turn it into a fun game of foreplay, sex, and cleaning? You will get so much done and feel so much better in the end.

7. A man's annoying habits affect women's interest in sex.

Things such as: the way men chew, burp, fart, leave the toilet seat up, leave their underwear or socks around, scratch their testicles, and use sweaty arm pits as a way to show off their manliness affects our interest in sex. When we first started dating, we may have been able to overlook these habits or maybe our men were doing them less often. But after ten years, these things matter. If men want more sex, they need to take care of these issues.

And because getting a Brazilian bikini wax or shaving our bodies all of the time is pure torture, men should show some appreciation by trimming their nose and ear hairs, and their privates, taking showers, using cologne, and so on. If men take care of themselves and their appearance, it will pay off in the bedroom!

8. Women fake orgasms for the sake of expediency and a man's ego.

Women fake orgasms and pleasure for the sake of expediency and the male ego. An orgasm seems to be very important for men because it tells them when the sexual encounter is not only over but successfully over. Sex is almost like a sport, a competition, and the orgasm is the win.

Yet studies consistently show that only 30 percent of women have orgasms from intercourse alone and about 30 percent have never had an orgasm at all. Because the majority of women don't have an orgasm easily, a lot of women fake it. Why do they fake it?

Well, in a way, the focus on orgasm is one of the worst things that happened to sex. Wanting to give your partner an orgasm is a great thought, but what happens when your partner (for whatever reason) can't have one? The frustration, pressure, and anxiety set in for both partners because the thought that comes to mind is: "You'd better come, or it's going to make me feel as if I can't please you!"

That's a lot of pressure. So women fake orgasms (although they shouldn't) either not to hurt men's feelings or to get them to finish up faster because the women are not in the mood or they are bored. In my opinion, in the spirit of honesty and better sex, we should, however, stop this ancient practice.

The best way to reset your thinking on this is: first, rather than focus on the orgasm, focus on what is pleasurable, and second, accept the idea that it is okay to simply pleasure your partner without having to have an orgasm at the same time. We also don't need to have an orgasm every time. We are okay with it, as long as men know it doesn't always have to do with their performance and as long as they are game to do whatever we need when we are ready for one. The important part is for us to speak up when we want one.

9. **"The vagina is a birth canal. The vulva is a gold mine." (Kim Catrall on esquire.com)**

We all have read, heard, or even perpetuated myths such as size matters or the importance of finding the G-spot. I don't know how a man would learn all of this because most of it comes through practice and experimenting and all of the stars aligning on the right day, at the right time, and in the right place. In case you don't know by now, sexual pleasure for a woman is a complex equation.

Of course, the sad part is that all of this seems like a lot of work and for some women, it really does not matter that much. What men need to do is ask their women for honest feedback and to actually listen to them, but until then, let me give you a hint: the clitoris is what matters, so focus on that!

10. **Women overanalyze everything down to punctuation, tone of voice, looks, and we do it during sex too, which pretty much kills sex every time.**

Although a married woman seems to be more tolerant about various things that the husband does because she is used to him, his way of thinking, and his mannerisms, it doesn't mean she can ignore his actions completely.

Even when she is in the bedroom, she can analyze his behavior (his behavior at the present time or his behavior two days ago). This makes it very difficult for her to relax and enjoy the ride. We are way too much into our heads and have difficulty enjoying pure physical sensations. "Analysis paralysis" is the name of the losing game. Men, help your woman relax and get out of her head. The winning game is all about patience, communication, and perhaps some good wine!

9
Final Thoughts

Well, who would have thought that sex in two minutes would be a marriage saver? Honestly, we all know that two-minute-sex during dating or the honeymoon is embarrassing and generally not a positive thing, but as the world turns and we evolve in our relationships and in our communication, two minutes can make or break your marriage.

In the spirit of consistency, I have designed this book to be short so that it can be a quick read (just a little longer than two minutes). I prefer to make this experience less about reading and more about practicing. Moreover, I have tried to keep it fair and balanced for both men and women and to truly consider both perspectives.

Of course, in that spirit of fairness, I know I have focused primarily on one dynamic in a marriage, specifically the one where the woman has a lower sex drive than the man. I know this does not speak for everyone. There are women (wives) who are struggling with in a sexless marriage due to a husband with a lower sex drive. And for that, I will have to write another book to pay full attention to the complexity of that situation.

For now, I am confident that *the 2-minute solution* highlighted in this book will provide a quick and viable solution for most families that are willing to try it. As much as I believe that anyone can benefit from reading this book, I can't stress enough that this method is best for partners who trust each other, truly still care about each other, and truly care about accommodating each other's needs.

I wrote this particularly for busy couples with incongruent schedules, tired parents with small children, and couples who, for one reason or another, have hit a rough patch. Yet, I have also found my method to be beneficial for individuals with premature ejaculation and people with chronic illnesses or chronic pain.

The sex and communication practices recommended in this book are all commonsense exercises, nothing earth-shattering, but together these could make a huge difference in your marriage. Time and time again, relationships are broken due to poor communication and sexual difficulties. Sometimes, couples go to therapy, but most of the time, they go to their friends, coworkers, pastors, the bookstore, and the Internet. Sometimes, they end up suffering from depression, alcohol abuse, porn addiction, and extramarital affairs because they feel their needs are not being met at home.

Time and time again, people make the mistake of equating their sex drive with the quality of their relationship. Sometimes, these may be related, but most of the time, one's sex drive is simply correlated to gender differences, the number of years in a relationship, and the amount of stress in one's life. Despite cultural, religious, pharmacological, and societal attempts to even out gender differences, the truth is that generally speaking, the sex drive is different for men and women.

Based on the research I have read, my experience with many couples in therapy, and my own personal experiences, I truly believe that men and women are different in terms of sexuality. I don't see it as a bad thing. I just see it as a fact of life - a fact of life that we should accept, instead of fight; a fact of life that we should learn to work around, not lie about or ignore in the hope that it will go away.

Real intimacy does not naturally happen. It takes some effort to achieve and maintain. It comes to those who are willing to engage in and be patient through the roller-coaster of hormones, honesty, and disagreements, but it is well worth the effort. Falling out of lust or romantic love isn't the end of a relationship, unless you let it become so. With patience, nurturance, and practice, it could be the beginning of a whole new chapter.

References

Bader, E., & Pearson, P. (2000). Tell Me No Lies: How to Stop Lying to Your Partner-And Yourself-In the 4 Stages of Marriage. St. Martin's Griffin: New York.

Baumeister, R.F., Catanese, K.R., & Vohs, K.D. (2001). Is there a gender difference in strength of sex drive? Theoretical views, conceptual distinctions, and a review of relevant evidence. Personality and Social Psychology Review. 5, 3, 242-273.

Beck, J.G., Bozman, A.W., & Qualtrough, T. (1991). The experience of sexual desire: Psychological correlates in a college sample. Journal of Sex Research, 28, 443-456.

Canner, L. (2009). Orgasm, Inc.

Elliott. S., & Umbersom, D. (2008). The Performance of desire: Gender and sexual negotiation in long-term marriages. Journal of Marriage and the Family, 70 (2), 391-406.

Ellis, B.J., & Symons, D. (1990). Sex differences in sexual fantasy: An evolutionary psychological approach. Journal of Sex Research, 27, 527-555.

Fisher, Helen (2004). Why we love: The nature and chemistry of romantic love. Henry Holt and Company, LLC, New York.

Fisher, H. E., Aron, A., Mashek, D., Li, H., & Brown, L.L. (2002). Defining the brain systems of lust, romantic attraction, and attachment. Archives of Sexual Behavior, 31, 5, 413-419.

Julien, D., Bouchard, C., Gagnon, M., & Pomerleau, A. (1992). Insiders' views of marital sex: A dyadic analysis. Journal of Sex Research, 29, 343-360.

Laumann E. O., Gagnon, J. H., Michael, R.T., & Michaels, S. (1994). The social organization of sexuality: Sexual Practices in the United States. Chicago: University of Chicago Press.

Lazarus, A. (2001). Marital Myths Revisited: A Fresh Look at two dozen mistaken beliefs about marriage. Atascadero, California: Impact Publishers, Inc.

Leitenberg, H. and Henning K. (1995). Sexual fantasy. Psychological bulletin, 117, 469-496.

Perel, Esther (2003). Erotic Intelligence. Psychotherapy Networker, Inc., May/June.

Perel, Esther (2006). When Three Threatens Two. Psychotherapy Networker, Sept/Oct, 58-63

Robinson, K. M. & Smith, M.W. (2014). 10 Surprising Health Benefits of Sex. Retrieved from: www.webmd.com/sex-relationships/guide/sex-and-health.

Schnarch, D. (2009). Passionate Marriage. W.W. Norton & Company: New York.

Voydanoff, P. & Donnelly, B.W. (1999). The inter-section of time in activities and perceived unfair-ness in relation to psychological distress and marital quality. Journal of Marriage and the Fami-ly, 61, 739-751.

Weiner Davis, Michele (2003). The Sex-Starved Marriage. Simon & Schuster: New York.

65962979R00058

Made in the USA
Lexington, KY
30 July 2017